Uthman Ibn Affan

(May Allah be pleased with him)

The Third Caliph of Islam

Sr. Nafees Khan

GOODWORD

Uthman (ra) was born around 576 C.E. in Taaif. Thus he was about six years younger than the Prophet Muhammad (pbuh). Both his parents, Affan and Urwa, were distant relatives of the Prophet (pbuh), Uthman received a formal education and was one of the few people in Makkah who could read and write.

Affan, a very rich merchant, died when Uthman (ra) was just twenty years old. Uthman, who inherited a great deal of wealth at his father's death, followed his father's profession. His straightforwardness combined with his ability to trade soon made him the richest person amongst the Quraish. He came to be known as 'Uthman Ghani' (Uthman the Rich). But he was best known for his modesty and good character. The Prophet Muhammad (pbuh) once said, "Uthman is the most modest of my Companions!" Even before becoming a Muslim, he never gambled or drank wine. He was an honest man and this was reflected in all his business and social dealings. He led a simple life and was regularly engaged in helping others and in doing social work to assist hundreds of widows, orphans and the poor. He was also helpful and kind towards his relatives. All this testified to his nobility of character.

Uthman (ra) was also famous for his handsome looks. In

spite of his wealth and good looks, he went out of his way to make sure that his behaviour did not hurt anyone. He was not at all arrogant. On the contrary, he was soft spoken and never tried to impose his views on others. All these qualities made him a popular and well-liked person.

Even before he accepted Islam, Uthman (ra) had great admiration for the Prophet Muhammad (pbuh) and would often seek his advice.

Abu Bakr and Uthman (ra) were close friends. They would frequently discuss the purpose of creation. When the Prophet Muhammad (pbuh) declared his mission, Uthman (ra) called on Abu Bakr (ra). Both men talked about it and Abu Bakr (ra) informed his friend that he had already accepted Islam. Abu Bakr (ra) then encouraged his friend to do so too. Both went to see the Prophet (pbuh). Uthman (ra) did not hesitate to take the *Shahada*. (Article of Faith: "There is no deity but Allah and Muhammad is His servant and Messenger.") From then on he became a very devout Muslim and remained so until his death.

The Quraish reacted violently to Uthman's (ra) conversion to Islam. Even his relatives turned against

him, but he stood firm in his new faith. The Prophet Muhammad (pbuh) appreciated his sacrifices and gave Uthman (ra) his daughter Ruqayyah (ra) in marriage.

The conditions in Makkah were becoming very difficult for the Muslims. The boycott by the Quraish added to their misery. So Uthman and Ruqayyah (ra) asked the Prophet for his permission to leave Makkah for Abyssinia. He acceded to their request, gave them his blessings and prayed for their safety. At the time of their departure he said, "After the Prophet Lut, Uthman is the first to migrate with his family in the way of Allah SWT." Very shortly thereafter, some other Muslims followed them to Abyssinia.

In Abyssinia, Allah blessed Uthman (ra) and Ruqayyah (ra) with a son, whom they named Abdullah. Two years later, they returned to Makkah, having heard that the

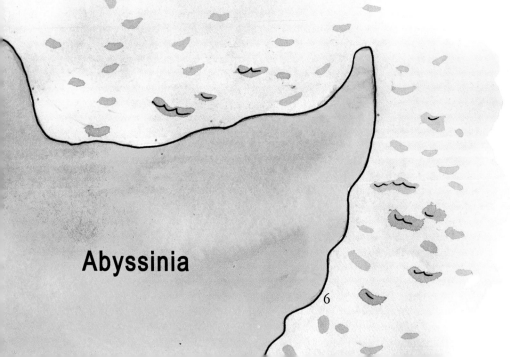

Abyssinia

Arabia

conditions for the Muslims had improved. Upon their arrival, they found out that the information they had received was incorrect.

During his stay in Makkah, Uthman spent most of his time in the company of the Prophet Muhammad (pbuh). He freed several slaves and continued to help the poor, especially during the social boycott imposed upon the Muslims by the Quraish.

In 622 C.E, he and Ruqayyah (ra) migrated again but this time to Madinah. They number among the very few people who ever had the honour of migrating twice for the sake of Allah. In Madinah, Uthman's (ra) business started to flourish and he soon became one of the richest people there as well.

When the Muhajirs first came to Madinah, they had great difficulty in getting drinking water. There was just one well and its owner would not allow Muslims to draw any water unless they paid a high price for it. The Prophet Muhammad (pbuh) asked, "Who is there who will buy this well for the Muslims? Allah will reward him with a fountain in Paradise." Uthman (ra) responded immediately. He bought the well for twenty thousand dirhams and donated it to the Muslims.

After the Prophet Muhammad (pbuh) migrated to Madinah, he visited Uthman (ra) and Ruqayyah (ra) frequently and enjoyed playing with his grandson, Abdullah. The couple were content and lead a happy life. Alas, their happiness was short-lived. In 624 C.E. after a brief illness, Ruqayyah (ra) passed away. Uthman (ra) was grief-stricken. Realizing that he was no longer a son-in-law of the Prophet made him even sadder. The Prophet Muhammad (pbuh) sensed this. About a year later, the Prophet gave his second daughter, Umm Kulthum (ra) in

marriage to Uthman (ra). He told his daughter that he found a resemblance in Uthman to his forefather Ibrahim. Thus Uthman (ra) earned the title of "Dhun Nurain", which means "the possessor of two lights." He was called this because he was married to two of the Prophet's (pbuh) daughters. Umm Kulthum (ra) loved Abdullah and took good care of him.

When Masjid un Nabi could not accommodate the growing number of Muslims, the Holy Prophet was obliged to ask, "Who is there to pay for the extension of this Masjid?" Again it was Uthman (ra) who stepped forward to take the responsibility.

Whenever help was needed, Uthman (ra) never hesitated to donate generously to the cause of Islam. On one occasion, Uthman's (ra) contribution was the largest. He gave one thousand camels, fifty horses and one thousand pieces of gold. When the Prophet Muhammad (pbuh)

saw what Uthman (ra) had given, he gave him the tidings of Paradise and said, "Whatever Uthman does from this day on will do him no harm!"

This happy marriage of Uthman (ra) and Umm Kulthum (ra) did not last long either. Umm Kulthum (ra) died six

years after her marriage in 630, C.E., without having had any children. Her father led the funeral prayers. Earlier, Abdullah had died at about the age of eight, two years after his own mother's death. Abdullah's funeral prayer was also led by the Prophet (pbuh). Uthman (ra) clung to the fond memories of both Ruqayyah (ra) and Umm Kulthum (ra) for the rest of his life.

In 639 C. E., during the caliphate of Umar (ra), there was a famine in Arabia that caused the people great hardship. When a caravan brought in a large shipment of grains that belonged to Uthman (ra), the merchants offered to buy it at double the price, which would have given Uthman (ra) a huge profit. They were told that he had already made a deal at a much higher price. The merchants were curious to know who had made such an offer. Uthman (ra) informed them that it was Allah SWT. After that, he distributed the entire stock amongst the needy.

Uthman (ra) was one of the few people who wrote down *ayat* (verses) of the Quran at the time they were revealed. He had also memorized the whole of the Quran. Even after the death of the Prophet Muhammad (pbuh), Uthman (ra) was held in high esteem by the Companions because of his noble nature and closeness to the Holy Prophet. He served as an advisor during the caliphates of Abu Bakr (ra) and Umar (ra).

While lying on his deathbed, and after much thought, Umar (ra) appointed six of the Prophet's most prominent

Companions to elect the next Caliph. To all of them, the Prophet had given the tidings of Paradise.

This committee of six gave Abdul Rahman bin Auf (ra) (one of the committee members) the task of selecting the leader. He interviewed several people, including the Bedouin chiefs who were in Madinah to attend Umar's (ra) funeral. He analyzed their answers, took into consideration the views of the public and prayed to Allah SWT for guidance before making up his mind.

Abdul Rahman bin Auf (ra) selected Uthman Ibn Affan (ra) and told him, "Promise that you will act according to the commandments of the Quran and the example set by

the Holy Prophet and his two Caliphs." Uthman pledged, "I promise to do that to the best of my knowledge and ability!" While he was speaking, the awareness of this great responsibility made his body shiver. Thus, at the age of seventy, in 644 C.E, Uthman (ra) became the third Caliph of Islam. People reacted favorably to Uthman's (ra) election.

After accepting the position, Uthman (ra) gave several directives setting guidelines for the heads of various departments and warned them that Allah would cause them to be replaced with others if they abused their authority.

The civil officers were given
the following guidelines:

".....Allah requires the administrators to
be the well-wishers and protectors of the
people. You are not just officers but protectors
as well. Learn about people's problems and help
in solving them. Ensure that there is a balance
between the duties and the rights of the
people.....whatever promises are made, even to
enemies, should be respected."

The officers of the military were told, "You are
to protect the life and property of both Muslims
and non-Muslims. The laws made hitherto
under Umar (ra) were made as a result of
consultations, therefore do not breach them."

The tax collectors were advised, "Allah enjoins
justice, therefore, be just and fair to all. Be

honest and pay particular attention to the orphans and the poor. See that the people are not taxed beyond their capacity. Do not oppress or harass the people."

And the general public was also reminded, "Follow Islam faithfully and do not introduce any *bid'ah* (innovations). Remain united, make sure that unity is maintained at all costs and hold on tightly to the 'Rope of Allah'." In another sermon he encouraged people to do as many good deeds as possible before death knocked on their doors.

In 650 C.E., concerns were raised about the recitation of the Quran. The Iraqis recited it in one way and the

Syrians in another way. The people of Kufa were reciting it in yet another way. This was causing a dispute. As usual, Uthman (ra) brought the matter before the senior Companions for consultation. They agreed that a standardized text of the Quran had to be prepared to avoid further disputes that might cause division amongst the people. A committee was formed and entrusted with this sacred task. So he had the distinction of uniting the Muslim community on a uniform version of the Quran.

During the Caliphate of Abu Bakr (ra), the Quran had been compiled under

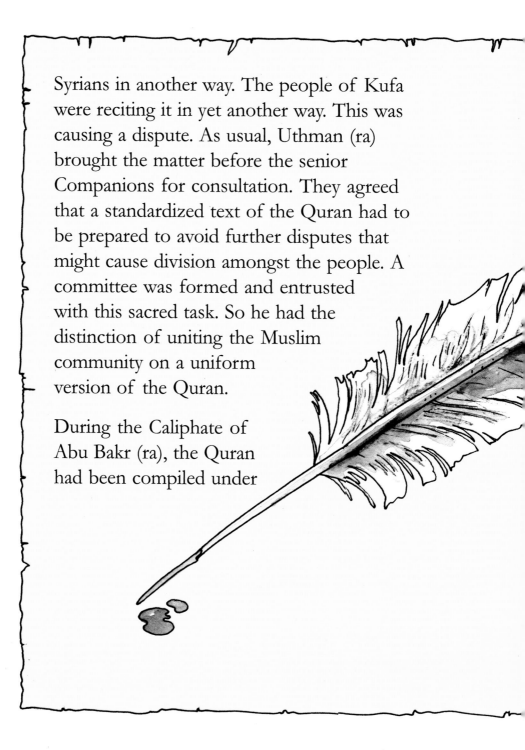

strict guidelines in the form of a book. This original copy was first kept in the custody of Ayesha (ra) and later on in that of Hafsa (ra), both wives of the Prophet Muhammad (pbuh).

The committee members were: Zaid bin Thabit, (one of the original main scribes during the Prophet's lifetime), Abdullah bin Zubair, Saeed bin Al 'As and Abdur Rahman bin Auf. Occasionally, Uthman (ra) had also performed this task as well. After the committee had completed its task, they read out this version to the gatherings of Muhajirs and Ansars three times. It was also compared with the original copy and no discrepancies were found. Uthman (ra), being a 'Hafiz' himself, double checked for accuracy and approved it. Copies of this edition were prepared and distributed to all the provinces. Thus, Uthman (ra) had the honour of preserving the original Quran that has remained intact to this day!

It was Uthman (ra) who started the tradition of supplying free meals to everyone during Ramadan at *Iftaar* (breaking of fast) time. The *mu'azzins* (those who called the people to prayers) started receiving salaries. For

the convenience of the people, the second call, was introduced for Friday prayers.

Uthman (ra) was very active in building projects and doing things to improve the daily lives of the *Ummah* (community). Uthman (ra) was the first Caliph to have the Masjid un Nabi and the Grand Masjid in Makkah extended and beautified. As many as five thousand 'masajid' were also built and arrangements were made for their upkeep.

Hundreds of canals and wells were dug to increase the water supply and to develop agriculture. Guesthouses were built in the big cities. It was Uthman (ra) who decided that Jeddah should be the site for the new

Masajid

Canal

Wells

seaport, as it was closer to Makkah than the port of Shusba.

A naval force was established for the first time after Uthman (ra) reluctantly gave permission to face the Roman navy that attacked the Muslims at every opportunity. Eventually, under Ameer

Rest Houses

Port

Muawiyah and Abdullah bin Sarah, the Muslim navy became a powerful force to reckon with and remained so for several centuries. During his caliphate, Islamic rule was consolidated in Persia and Egypt and spread to the whole of North Africa and also across some parts of Spain. It even spread to Azerbaijan, Armenia, Kabul and Ghazni.

The economic policies of Uthman (ra) brought prosperity to the people. Some very quickly became rich and this became a source of resentment for others. Contrary to the Islamic teaching of brotherhood, some of the Quraish started developing a sense of superiority, thus weakening the bond of unity.

By the middle of Uthman's caliphate, most of the senior

companions had passed away and the faith of the younger generation was not as strong as that of the previous one. Islam had enjoined obedience to its leaders but there were some who even started questioning the authority of the Caliph, while others spread wrong information about him. Uthman (ra) did not take a salary from the state. He supported his needy relatives and kinsmen financially by drawing upon his own wealth. Yet, people quite erroneously believed that he helped his relatives and kinsmen by dipping into the funds of the *Bait ul Maal* (Public Treasury).

Uthman (ra) had continued the policy of Umar (ra), by not distributing the conquered lands amongst the soldiers. The previous owners had the right to keep their own property. The army demanded that Uthman (ra) should change this policy. Discontent quietly spread when he did not give in to the army's demand. Later on, the unhappy soldiers indirectly supported the rebels.

Umar (ra) had ruled with a firm hand, but people took advantage of Uthman (ra), who was very mild-natured and kind-hearted, often overlooking the faults of others. It was the officers, governors and people whom he loved and trusted the most who took advantage of his good nature to lay the blame for their own shortcomings upon him. This created unrest in the provincial capitals and made it easy for those who had grudges against Uthman (ra) to convince people that the Caliph was the root cause of their complaints.

Uthman (ra) did his best to control the situation and satisfy the dissenters. He addressed the people in the Masjid un Nabi, patiently explaining his 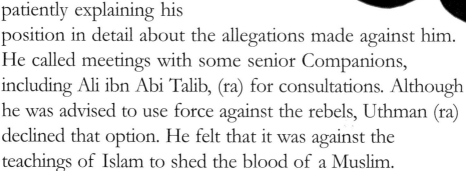 position in detail about the allegations made against him. He called meetings with some senior Companions, including Ali ibn Abi Talib, (ra) for consultations. Although he was advised to use force against the rebels, Uthman (ra) declined that option. He felt that it was against the teachings of Islam to shed the blood of a Muslim.

Opposition to the Caliph gained momentum and was becoming dangerous. He was determined not to use force at any cost and was prepared to risk his own life to avoid division and bloodshed amongst the Muslims. He had heard the Prophet Muhammad (pbuh) say that there would be no end to a civil war once it started. Uthman (ra) did not want to be the one to start it off.

The last sermon of Uthman (ra) was highly significant. He said:

"The truth is that you are in this world merely to prepare for the next world. Allah never intended that you should be attracted by the world. This world will not last; the

hereafter alone will be eternal. Therefore, you should not be proud of anything in this world. Beware that you do not become forgetful of the next world. Prefer the hereafter to this world, for you have ultimately to return to Allah. Always fear Allah….."

In the month of Shawwal, 35 Hijrah (656 C.E) three armed groups of rebels came to Madinah from Egypt, Kufa and Basra. They studied the situation in Madinah and, when they realized that there would be no resistance, they surrounded the Caliph's house.

Uthman (ra) was not allowed to leave the house to go to the Masjid un Nabi for prayers. Even food and water were withheld. The siege continued for 40 days. Uthman (ra) was convinced that his time for martyrdom had arrived as predicted by his beloved Prophet (pbuh). Hence he made some preparations. It was Friday, 18th Zilhijjah and he decided to fast, freed twenty slaves, put on new clothes and started reciting the Quran.

Hasan, Husain (ra), grandsons of the Prophet Muhammad (pbuh), Abdullah bin Zubair (ra) and other youths were guarding the front of the Caliph's house. Some rebels forced their way through the back and brutally assassinated the 82-year old third Caliph.

Uthman (ra) was an extremely religious man who would spend his nights praying. At night, he used to fetch the water for the *wudu* himself instead of waking up his servants, as he believed that they deserved their rest. He liberated a slave every Friday.

Uthman (ra) was kind, peace-loving and tolerant. He followed Islam strictly and his love for the Prophet Muhammad (pbuh) had no bounds. He was one of the first to memorize the Quran from cover to cover. He regarded the responsibility of the caliphate as a sacred

duty and believed that he was answerable to Allah. No wonder the Prophet Muhammad (pbuh) had given him the glad tidings of Paradise not once but three times. Therefore, it may be said that rebellion against Uthman (ra) was a rebellion against Islam. May Allah be pleased with him, ameen.